Day Job

poems by

Jan Ball

Finishing Line Press
Georgetown, Kentucky

Day Job

Copyright © 2020 by Jan Ball
ISBN 978-1-64662-192-7 First Edition
All rights reserved under International and Pan-American Copyright Conventions. No part of this book may be reproduced in any manner whatsoever without written permission from the publisher, except in the case of brief quotations embodied in critical articles and reviews.

ACKNOWLEDGMENTS

massage therapist, *Pennine Ink* (U.K.)
Augsburg Pedicure, *Voice of Eve*
Undertakers at Lightning Ridge, *All the Sins* (U.K.)
play street for the needy, *Indiana Voice Journal*
yearly physical, *The Silt Reader*
treatment, *Pamplemousse*
Nonno Vincenzo's New Job, *ABZ*
Joaquin Says Mass the First Time in English, *California Quarterly*
Reynaldo, *Toasted Cheese*
Wall Street Farmer, *Foliate Oak Review*
Uber Driver, *The Magnolia Review*

Publisher: Leah Maines
Editor: Christen Kincaid
Cover Art: Quentin Ball
Author Photo: Quentin Ball
Cover Design: Elizabeth Maines McCleavy

Printed in the USA on acid-free paper.
Order online: www.finishinglinepress.com
also available on amazon.com

Author inquiries and mail orders:
Finishing Line Press
P. O. Box 1626
Georgetown, Kentucky 40324
U. S. A.

Table of Contents

Hair Stylist 1

massage therapist 2

Augsburg Pedicure 3

Undertakers at Lightning Ridge 5

Simon's Lecture 6

Red-headed Researcher 8

English for UAE Soldiers 9

play street for the needy 10

No Refuge 13

ENT 14

yearly physical 15

treatment 16

Nonno Vincenzo's New Job 17

It's Personal 18

Joaquin Says Mass the First Time in English 19

Gig at Cook County Jail 20

Reynaldo 21

Residents 23

odious chores 25

Housekeeping at Harbourside Apartment Hotel ... 26

Wall Street Farmer 27

Uber Driver 28

Hair Stylist

She spots him as soon as she enters
the wedding reception room
where, to her, he sparkles and glows
from the back like Disney's Fantasia
through the eyes of a child. He could
be Elvis with red hair for the charisma
of his ginger coloring.

As she nonchalantly walks over to him
at the bar, she imagines her comb gliding
along his scalp while she lovingly calms
the unruly strands, teases out tangles,
      snips here,
                snips there,

smoothing each golden hair above the ears,
watering down the cow-lick at his forehead,

a different challenge from slathering color
on faded clumps and folding them in tin foil
to create highlights for blondes, covering
gray roots on brunettes, or bouffanting
silvery female clients.

She introduces herself, but resists picking
at the few stray red hairs on his jacket
lapel until later.

massage therapist

You have just returned from massaging
the Northwestern Swim Team in competition
at Ohio State, manipulating those toned, strong
bodies like elastic pizza dough with your capable
hands, smoothing their lateralis, trapezius and
quadriceps muscle groups, as you explained
to me, so they can speed through the chlorinated
water as efficiently as submarines, but now I lay
on your massage table, a sack of flour by comparison
(although I do work out three times a week and play
tennis), gobs of cellulite on my thighs, chicken skin
hanging off my upper arms, wrinkled, fatigued,
but when you knead my shoulders and score my back,
I am like your swimmers, eighteen again, pliant and
smooth, swimming the entire length of the pool.

Augsburg Pedicure

Not the pirhana pedicure
of London where little fish
nibble our tough callouses
or the luxurious soakings
in hot, gardenia-scented
water in an American salon,

instead in a cobbled alley
in Augsburg, away from cafés
in Fuggersplatz, a sign says
NAILS so I follow it to an open
door where a young Vietnamese
woman in very short shorts and
a black and white baseball cap
with writing I don't understand
even though it is supposedly
English, leads me up a staircase
to an empty area except for two
gray chairs and says *sit*, then
brings a wooden bucket of tepid
water and sits on the other chair
while she slides the bucket
in front of me and indicates
that I should submerge my feet
in it.

As she arranges my softened soles
on a cushion between her legs, we
hesitantly try to talk. Because I have
no German except *bitte* or *danke* and
because I say, enunciating words
slowly, that I taught English
to Vietnamese refugees in Australia,
gesturing *boat*, she retrieves words
that I know from her pronunciation
are from her childhood, so we
are able to communicate a little.

She snips the overgrown cuticles, clips
the toenails that make holes in my socks
and massages my feet and ankles
so tenderly that in a beergarden
where we go for dinner, the flies think
that I'm a bakery.

A buxom manicurist with Cleopatra
eyes, comes up the stairs and tells me
that she learned English from girls
she worked with then goes to the WC,
I presume, and a good-looking
Vietnamese man in cargo pants
converses in their tonal language
with repartee that brings out harsh
sounds and sly, sidewise looks
from my pedicurist.

I pay the thirty Euros with tip
as my pedicurist struggles to say,
I want ideas, you, gesturing at her head.

Instead, I say *goodbye* but give her
an American hug before I walk away.

Undertakers at Lightning Ridge

In a town with an opal mine,
but without a funeral home,
amateur Australian morticians
don't know how to embalm,
but some study how to beautify,
most recently the corpse
of Valerie Van Emmerick,
a thrice-married, rabbit-hunting
miners' cook who had knocked
down a man in a fistfight.

The opal miner who took
the beautician's course arranges
her hair in curls and applies
make-up after he and his mate
lift her hefty body into the white,
satin-padded coffin, presumably
washing their large hands first
and taking off their muddy boots.

After a brief memorial service
in the bowling club, a retired minister
asks if any mourners want to speak.
One tells how Valerie had *taken
a miner out* at a miner's meeting,
obviously a pub-favorite story.

Because of the heavy seasonal rains,
the grave the miners dig for Valerie
is flooded, so they take the coffin
to the new mortuary that once was
a Lion's Club. Until the rains let up
and the grave dries out, her body
remains in the refrigerator
that stored beer.

Simon's Lecture

Simon has brought one suit to London
to address The Institute of Chartered
Accountants of England and Wales,
so when we meet our British friends,
Judith and Edward, for afternoon tea
at the Savoy, he wears the suit without
a tie as many men do in style now.

Like in the movies, there are tiered
trays of cucumber sandwiches, egg
salad, smoked salmon, all without
their crusts, Scottish scones raisin-
dotted on the top tier, with little
Royal Dalton bowls of lemon curd
and cream, then platefuls of other
scrumptious pastries served with
plentiful cups of tea that we have
selected individually: jasmine, Earl
Grey and English Breakfast, poured
by a suave British waiter who could
be Benedict Cumberbatch, practicing
for a role different than Alan Turing
in *The Imitation Game*.

Meanwhile, our friend Judith reapplies
her red lipstick twice stretching her
mouth vertically in a compact mirror
like Munch's *Scream*. Our jetlag kicks
in so we excuse ourselves and kiss
farewells the European way on either
cheek, but also exchange American hugs.

The day of Simon's lecture, he has to start
early with breakfast at eight then two videoed
interviews. He returns to our suite at The Andaz
Hotel for a break and says, "Guess what! When
they videoed me for the interviews, I realized
I had red lipstick on my left lapel, so I told
the cameramen to focus on my right shoulder.

On the way back to the hotel, I tried
cleaners around Bishopsgate to remove
the stain, but they all send their laundry
out so I'll have to wear it this way
for the lecture tonight."

I exclaim, "Judith!" then observe,
"No one will see it up on the dais."

Later, when I take the elevator
downstairs with Simon as he
leaves for his lecture, we tell
another passenger what happened.
He smiles and says, "Likely story."

Red-headed Researcher

"Rudy", you call
the red-headed woodpecker
rat-tat-tatting
against the telephone pole
this morning at our farm.

It's so like you to name things,
animals or concepts:
"Molie" the mole,
"Randolph" the rabbit,
"J Curve", or "S Curve",
identify anomalies,
explore the dimensions
of any topic, sublime
or mundane,

rat-tat-tatting
your position,
not unlike
the red-headed woodpecker
at the telephone pole
furiously
uncovering insects
rather than patterns
and trends in the data
in the ungraphed country air.

NB: Thanks to Professors Peter Easton
and Paul Michas for helping me
with the statistics.

English for UAE Soldiers

I read bedtime stories
to the Lebron James-
fit-men to demonstrate
how we learn a language.

Stuffed into college desks
designed for slimmer students,
they almost nod off
        like tired children
with the rhythm and
        occasional rhyme
of "once upon a time."

I encourage them to read
to their own children
in bland English
or musical Arabic,
and try to stimulate discussion
asking, "Did your parents read
to you when you were young?"

Yusef, probably the brightest
of the battalion, shares
that his parents were illiterate
yet here he is learning English
at an American university,
he wryly muses.

I taught the soldiers English,
and they taught me how to
kill a man: Just stick two fingers
in the soft space between
his clavicles and push
until he dies.

play street for the needy

That late sixties summer in New Haven,
a few months after I left the convent
when 25,000 other nuns left, too (I later
learned), three of us took our first flight
to Connecticut: Judy, formerly Sister
John Ann, Sara, a second grade teacher
at my last convent appointment, and me,
my hair grown out, in a beehive, an external
manifestation in lacquer and swirls
of my mind after seven years as a nun.

Tall Larry set up a volleyball net on the closed-
off street we were hired to pied-piper-attract
the neighborhood children to, draw them away
from more sinister past-times. When not playing
volleyball, we rested on the local prostitute's
steps as men discreetly lined up to the left
of us on pay-day mornings. I had to apologize
to her when I slapped her son because he
repeatedly kicked my leg during rounds
of *ring around the rosie*.

Jerry, the handsome episcopal seminarian
from Yale Divinity School where we'd been
invited for discussion groups by the assistant
pastor, Tom, who was doing a P.h.D. there
and lived upstairs (he and his wife generously
cooked for us a few times), tried to seduce one
of us (it turned out he would have preferred
Sara) by bringing us a pineapple, behavior
alien to our association with Catholic priests,
and the Southern Black man I slow-danced
with at a church social drove past the parish
house where we were staying over and over
again in an old, gray Chevy with his friends
until we got Tom to ask that he stop hooting,
"Hey, babe, woo-woo!"

A portly Indian exchange teacher with
a receding hairline, also from Yale Divinity,
asked me to a curry dinner in his apartment.
I wore my new green corduroy suit that I
would later wear for passport photos. He
put his arm around me on the couch until I
started reminiscing about the convent then
he compulsively pulled at the buttons and
button-holes on his tweed jacket and changed
to psychologist mode. We ate the delicious
cauliflower curry in coconut gravy he'd
prepared, chatting for hours with strange
Indian music in the background. I had
a good time.

Meanwhile, little Sherilee, on the play street,
split her forearm on a sharp stone when she
fell on the asphalt playing *red rover* so we
wrapped her arm in a towel and rushed her
to the ER of the local hospital in our supervisor,
Wayne's car, and waited there until twilight
when interns finally stitched the gash. We
brought her to her house across from
the prostitute's where many people were
gathered for a prayer meeting, but we were
not invited in after we tapped on the screen
door even though Wayne was ethnically
acceptable.

Judy and I finally realized that blonde Sara
was connecting with Wayne when we heard
about them making out at a movie we were all
supposed to be supervising. After the adolescents
at the movie booed them, Sara decided she'd lost
respect so said she'd have to leave the street
supervision work early (you could change your
flights easier then), but before she left, Sara

convinced Judy and me to steal something
from the local A & P. Sara stole a pack of Kents;
Judy stole a banana and I stole a bottle of ketchup,
hiding it in my woven straw purse like so much
I hid then but remember now.

No Refuge

Jason is delighted to be in Sarasota using the folks' apartment
while he sails his catamaran competitively in the sparkling bay.
He hums "Dixie" as he skips down the stairs to the parking area,
but when he opens the driver's door of his parents' Camry,
he smells rotten fish. He is a trained mechanic so he pops
the hood to check the cabin air system.

He finds a deteriorating mouse with six pups clogging
the air flow to the body of the car. As he removes
the blockage, Jason assumes the mouse mom must
have looked for refuge when she sensed the approach
of Hurricane Michael but that she didn't make
a good choice to protect her young this time.

Unfortunately, this is not the end of the story.

Jason and his wife are notified in a lab report a few days
after the race that their foetus is carrying Edwards Disease:
that it may develop a small, abnormally shaped head,
a small jaw and mouth, long fingers that overlap
with undeveloped thumbs and clenched fists, low-set ears,
smooth feet with rounded soles, a cleft palate and a sac
outside the tummy where the intestines are held.

They will have to either terminate the pregnancy or keep
the infant alive in a deformed state until it usually dies
before a year.

ENT

The white-coated technologist says
my silver hearing aids will no longer
function in a crowded room; the test
shows sounds are fuzzy around
the edges like hearing underwater:
blub, blub, blub, and sounds will now
be just as indistinct.

She apologizes for the bad news, says
she's been giving it all day. Still, I
compliment her on her patent leather
shoes. It's not her fault my hearing
is deteriorating. I say, "I've looked
for shoes like that but just can't find
them anywhere."

She says she took them when her sister
died four years ago, and they were probably
seven years old then, says she'll look for
some for me and call me if she finds
what I am looking for.

yearly physical

Doctors no longer press my intestines
to determine how my digestive system
works, saying, "Does this hurt, does
that hurt," the way Dr. Vardaman used to
stretch his fingers across my abdomen
in his yellow hibiscus floral shirt, cold
watch on his wrist, ready to walk out
the examination room door for other
adventures at his St. Thomas hide-away,
as he told us, but now my downtown
doctor uses more technologically advanced
procedures, drawing blood like some
giant mosquito intern in a white coat,
afterwards arranging platelets under
a microscope or whatever they do
to determine how my liver is processing
all that alcohol I drank last night and whether
I have any Vietnamese parasites leaping around
my innards like ballet dancers from my vacation
last summer.

This morning before I get up, while staring
at the ceiling light fixture, I gingerly push
down at various points on my belly trying
to remember where my appendix is:
Dozing? Taking a shower? And whether
my gallbladder is still working at the food
processing factory, sitting on a stool
separating the nuts I ate yesterday from
their oil with a long-handled sieve, hairnet
over her frizzy hair to comply with health
standards, assuring that my body remains
ship-shape until my physical next year.

treatment

Maybe it was electro convulsion therapy
or electroshock treatments that made
the patients we served less expressive
than our aunts and uncles from farms
outside of Omaha, Nebraska, but what
did we know as *false prophets in black*,
as Sister Archeleus used to refer to us
when, as our novice mistress, she chose
some of us to serve dinner at the Sanitorium
that adjoined the motherhouse. We wore
black veils to replace the novitiate white
ones that we wore daily for our kitchen
carrot-scrapings, potato-peelings and
laundry work except when some of us left
the convent to sing *Dies Irae* at funeral
masses in Milwaukee Catholic churches
so being chosen to serve at the San seemed
like going to a birthday party by contrast.

Maybe it was recognizing the faces without
affect that jarred some remaining behavior
patterns in me that convent regulations hadn't
reached, not yet a *blank slate* like the aspirants
who entered at thirteen from elementary school.
I had seen the almost inert San patients submerged
in mud baths as my novice colleagues and I
collected their soiled hospital gowns and wrinkled
sheets.

Maybe the oatmeal treatment smell triggered
some reminiscence from the farm kitchen I had
left behind four years ago, the sad faces of the San
patients, the chicken and carrots we brought them
for dinner and took away congealed in gravy that
I thought about while chanting Divine Office
or moving my fingers from one rosary bead
to another before I felt I needed a warm towel
wrapped around myself back home in Omaha.

Nonno Vincenzo's New Job

Retired Nonno Vincenzo with his caterpillar
eyebrows has become a guard at the Chicago
Historical Society. So enthusiastic about his
duties, he has already been warned about
his gruff boxer voice and unrefined gestures
in trying to keep public school children
from trespassing into the cordoned-off areas
that protect furniture and stained glass designed
by Frank Lloyd Wright as well as a pocket watch
used by Abraham Lincoln and a Boeing Air
Transport stewardess uniform circa 1930.

After dinner, Ma and Pa whisper about how
Nonno appears to have been even more aggressive
in dealing with a large Greek man who resented
his domineering ways, both of them finally rolling
around on the polished marble floor, squawking
like belligerent cocks as they poked their fingers
up each others' nostrils and tried to twist
each other's earlobes (at least) the way they did
as children in *the old country* and certainly would
have been recorded on video camera today.

When Nonno returns from work, sans uniform,
to the meatball fragrant kitchen of his little
bungalow on Mohawk Street, he passes through
the concrete front yard where he grows basil
and oregano in ceramic pots but first he scans
the curb carefully to make sure no one has parked
in front of his house; otherwise, he would have to
slash the tires of the car even though it's
not snowing.

It's Personal

I hadn't told any of my students
at the tennis club that I was gay
so when Sara asked if she could
see me after class to ask me
a personal question, I was nervous.

The class had been the usual mix
of forehand, backhand, overheads,
volleys at the net and serves,
always fun with this group of older,
irreverent women with their smart,
double-meaning remarks.

I had almost forgotten that Sara
had asked to see me, but there she
was dawdling, tapping her tennis
racket on the floor after everyone else
filed out leaving a trail of inuendos.

I braced myself because she'd said
"personal question," but tried to act
natural, zipping up my track suit
jacket casually when I asked, "You
wanted to see me?"

Sara looked right at the center
of my face and replied, "George,
if you don't mind me asking.
Is that your real nose?"

Joaquin Says Mass the First Time in English

Accustomed to vowels that hover
on the aspirated language waves
of Andalucia, he nervously rolls
the English gravel around his mouth,
clicks the harsh consonant endings
against his front teeth then skips
the d and t sounds like stones
across the lake of his congregation,
The Lord be with you.

*Lamb of God who takes away the sins
of the world* causes him to lose the final
s on takes but the assembled community
so loves this humble, bearded man
who self-describes his poor hands and
poor life bringing them the body
and blood of their Christ that they are
not bothered by his poor English.

The final *Peace be with you,* almost
right, as the participants take hands
in friendship; the *p* and *b* ripple
the same in both languages, so he only
mispronounces the vowel *i* in *with*
articulating it the Spanish way to rhyme
with *heath*, but overcome with such delight
at his accomplishment, he floats out of
the sanctuary relieved, no longer worried
about getting the words perfectly correct.

Gig at Cook County Jail

The trio wears panty-hose today
and jackets with shoulder pads,
the Andrews Sisters' forties look
promising harmony:

> *Don't Sit Under the Apple Tree*
> *I Can Dream, Can't I*
> *Don't Fence Me In.*

The prison administrators have
suggested that after their presentation,
the ladies dance with criminals less
dangerous than the ones snickering
in the balcony, secure
                behind chicken wire.

Boogie Woogie Bugle Boy
in the background, Sheila,
adrenalinized after the spirited
rendition of her soprano part,
shouts like a teen at a rock
concert, "Would anyone like
to dance with us to the next song?"

Instead of the carefully hand-picked
group they expect, all the men,
except the killers in the balcony,
rush the stage with the enthusiasm
of Superbowl fans.

Fortunately, the guards exert order
immediately, rap-rap-rapping
their palms with their night sticks,
so the men line up as obediently
as soldiers, to take a turn dancing
with the three singers. "They're
great dancers," Sheila says later.

Reynaldo

I glimpse only the lower half of the painting
with the fore-shortened arms of Reynaldo,
the fish-monger, cutting raw pink fish
on a restaurant kitchen counter, from where
I sit at our dining room table glimpsing up
from cards,

—shuffle, deal, shuffle, deal—

after blue fin crabmeat garnish on Caesar
salad for dinner at home in Sarasota, Florida.

Last winter we admired the painting
displayed for sale on an outside wall
when we ate at Starfish, pelicans floating
in Sarasota Bay and great blue herons
flightlessly attached to boats like
hood ornaments, so when John returned
to Chicago briefly, I bought the painting
for him for his birthday.

While I negotiated the purchase with
the cashier, a man rushed out of the kitchen
grinning like a celebrity and after a warm
handshake, Reynaldo (I discovered)
offered to sign the back of the canvas
as if he were the painter.

Simultaneously, a woman emerged
smiling with I-phone poised
to photograph Reynaldo with me,
the two of them effusive as actors
portraying fishmongers who rehearse
their lines while trimming pompano,
grouper and soft shell crab as we eat
our lunchtime fish sandwiches—oblivious
of anyone behind the scenes preparing fish.

Back home, we see all of Reynaldo while
we prepare our dinner in our own kitchen:
chopping onions at the cutting board, stirring
the pumpkin soup, or only Reynaldo's arms
at the dining room table when we play cards

    clubs, diamonds, hearts, spades.

Residents

They have an average IQ
of fifty like an eight or nine-
year-old American child but
also the characteristics we know
them by: small chins, slanted eyes,
a flat nasal bridge and some have
strabismus which means both
eyes don't move together.

The Down Syndrome residents
of Misericordia, Chicago, don't
    take our lunch orders
    at their restaurant—
    The Greenhouse Inn;
female volunteers do in black pants
    and white shirts but a resident
brings a card to our table
with a list of specials and reads it
in a staccato computer voice
    staring into space
        like a blind person.

We help ourselves to tomato soup,
a specials list item, from the buffet
table but bring Carol's soup to her
since she is in a wheelchair,
physically challenged. Residents
with little people arms and legs bring
our orders to the table. After we finish
our soup and tuna or ham sandwiches,
another resident brings the dessert cart
and in a military tone, like the specials
speaker or, an announcer at a race track,
rat-tat-tats the names of desserts without
looking at us:

        coconut cake, éclair,
        butterscotch pudding
        strawberry shortcake
        and chocolate delight
but with good pronunciation for someone
who could have a protruding tongue
at one end of the spectrum, but
   probably
      has a large tongue
         in a small mouth
which is more common.

Later we peruse the gift shop
for handicrafts, Carol maneuvering
her wheelchair around display tables
like a Nascar driver trying to find
artwork done by residents. I buy
mainly blue primitive note cards
designed in-house, then leave
on time for my pilates appointment
   eager to share the details
        of my unusual lunch
with my instructor. Instead of
expressing surprise, however, she says,
"I know it well. My older brother Gary
was there for eighteen years, but he
   wouldn't
      have been able
         to serve you."

odious chores

Mother irons the laundry-Dad's
khaki work pants and shirts that
say *Don* on the breast pocket, our
summer-colorful blouses, bold orange,
red and green flowers scattered from
armpit to hem, then bends over
the plastic-lined wash basket and
exhales as loudly as a steam engine
going up a hill as her impatient fingers
pluck at the next item that she has
dampened with an andyworholic
coca-cola bottle with holes punched
in the cap. With a scowl, she smooths
a real cotton handkerchief on the flat
ironing board applying pressure with
the iron as if she were staunching
a wound before she wipes the sweat
from her neck with a wet washcloth.

Today, I iron my lavender-scented
clothes with a steam iron, one of
the household chores I choose to do;
my husband sends his dress shirts
to the cleaners and washes his knit
shirts himself on permanent press.
I've left the sound system on after
breakfast so I can enjoy the Fourth
of July music: The Grand Canyon
Suite then "Bess, you are my woman
now," sung by an excellent *basso
profundo*, the iron an ice skater across
my white linen pants and green silk
blouse while perspiration drips
rhythmically down my back which
I'll soon rehydrate with coconut
water.

Housekeeping at Harbourside Apartment Hotel

At four o'clock I call the front desk
and enquire if the cleaners are coming.
Suzanne (I find out later) answers
and tells me, "They're gone for the day,
but I can bring you fresh towels;
sometimes the tag on the doorknob
gets twisted in the breeze so switches
from MAKE UP THE ROOM to
          DO NOT DISTURB.

My blood starts to boil like making
Italian Spaghetti (as my family called pasta)
because one of the reasons that
we are leaving Sydney is that Australian
workers exert more power
over management than in the U.S.:
    strikes on the ferry,
    strikes on the trains,
so I sass back, "Not in this case."
What I don't say is that when I
returned from lunch I saw a cleaner
deliberately look at my doorknob
then sniff at me and make a decision
not to clean my room so she could
go home early, probably, to pick up
her kids from school or daycare.

A few minutes later, Suzanne
(her tag naming the voice
I heard) knocks on the door
with the towels and a big smile
on her face—as if we had
a housekeeper at home who changed
towels everyday, anyway!

Wall Street Farmer

The flowering pear tree I bought for *the man
who has everything* arrives in spring looking
like a broomstick, not exactly the arborist's
white petalled delight featured on the web
page of Andrea's nursery and even now,
in July, it still looks like a stick despite
tornado downpours and battleship proportions
of fertilizer. Nevertheless, small birds with
white breasts perch on top like Christmas
tree angels.

My fingertips still fragrant with the mint
I have been trying to control in my back
garden, one of the few plants this year's
epidemic rabbits have not devoured: parsley,
daisy and blanket flower salad, (We don't
dare plant carrots) but now that we've placed
a plastic brown owl from Farm King behind
the bee balm and sprinkled chili pepper
on the phlox and coreopsis, we might finally
have a garden that even visitors to Regent's
Park in London might admire and hopefully
will attract our adult children and their families
from Texas and Connecticut.

Meanwhile, Don will finish spraying Round-up
on the crab-grass that invades the gravel driveway,
"giving the impression that no one lives here."
I deadhead the marigolds, distribute breakfast
coffee grounds among the purple salvia, remove
raccoon scat from the side steps and water
the potted geraniums until it is time to drive
back to our high rise in Chicago.

Uber Driver

When I tell the Uber driver that the friend
I had a bowl of French onion soup and half
a chicken salad sandwich with at McNamara's
is dying of pancreatic cancer, he tells me
that his son died of cancer last year, that he
hasn't been able to pull himself together
since then, crying uncontrollably while
buying milk and eggs at Jewel, so his
therapist suggested that he drive for Uber.

We join the traffic on Chicago's I-94 which
is busy already at two o'clock and I reply
that many men wouldn't have the courage
to do therapy. He tells me that he's
a product of the projects. As he continues
to talk, we co-incidentally drive past North
Avenue and Halsted. He nods to the right
where the projects used to be, then nods
to the left saying, "I went to Lincoln High
School," and then I understand why
his speech is so articulate.

He continues the saga of his life saying, "I got
involved in gangs and ended up in penitentiary;"
he doesn't say *jail* but *penitentiary*. As an ESL
teacher, I am intrigued by his vocabulary as well
as his pronunciation, but suddenly wonder if all
of this is a scam to get a better tip now that you
can tip Uber on their website.

When we get to my high rise on Lake Michigan,
"the one with the awning," I reach to the front
seat to shake his hand and wish him luck. I tell
my doorman about how the Uber driver has
down-loaded on me. "Do I have a sign
on my forehead that says TALK TO ME?"
I ask. Harold says, "No, but maybe you could
think about becoming a bartender."

Jan started seriously writing poetry and submitting it for publication in 1998. Since then, she has had 317 poems accepted or published in the U.S., Australia, Canada, India, Ireland, Czech Republic and England. Published poems have appeared in: *ABZ, Atlanta Review, Calyx, Chiron, Main Street Rag*, and many other journals. Her poem, carwash, won the 2011 Betsy Colquitt Award for the best poem in a current issue of Descant, Fort Worth. Jan's poem "Loquat Jam" was awarded first place in the annual Loquat Festival of Port Ritchie, Florida (2018). Her two chapbooks, *Accompanying Spouse* (2011) and *Chapter of Faults* (2014), have both been published by Finishing Line Press. Jan's first full length poetry collection, *I Wanted To Dance With My Father*, was also published by Finishing Line Press (2017). Jan is a member of The Poetry Club of Chicago. Besides her poetry publications, she wrote a doctoral dissertation at the University of Rochester in 1996. The title is: *Age and Natural Order in Second Language Acquisition*.

Jan taught ESL at DePaul University in Chicago until recently. She lived in Australia for fifteen years with her Australian husband, Ray Ball. Her two children, Geoffrey and Quentin, were born in Brisbane. She is a twin to Jean Helmken and she was a Franciscan nun for seven years (Sister Jeanclare). When not writing poetry, working with her personal trainer at FFC, going to book group or traveling, Jan and her husband like to cook for friends. These background experiences infuse her poetry.

www.ingramcontent.com/pod-product-compliance
Lightning Source LLC
LaVergne TN
LVHW041515070426
835507LV00012B/1596